WINNIE'S WISDOM

GREAT TENNIS TRUTHS

FROM AN 'OLD' PRO

Winnie Gillaford

To Ann Hemphill (the
whole business!) Here's to
great future points

Wes Hotchkins

WINNIE'S WISDOM

GREAT TENNIS TRUTHS FROM AN 'OLD' PRO

By Winifred C. Gilliford

Illustrated by Wesley Hotchkiss

Crawford Press, Lancaster, PA

DEDICATION

To my mother, Frances Fronefield Gant,
a totally positive and truly disciplined person,
who had a huge influence in my life and the lives
of many others. Any success I achieved in my
lifetime can be attributed to her influence,
because there wasn't anything she thought I
couldn't try.

ACKNOWLEDGEMENTS

To Jerry Kinkead, without whose knowledge, expertise and generosity this project would never have become a book. For kitchen table sessions with the tape recorder, for transforming notes and tapes into printed paragraphs, typing, editing, organizing, designing and formatting; for being my business manager and friend.

To Wes Hotchkiss for understanding that tennis is about having fun and portraying that spirit with his wonderful, whimsical illustrations.

To Weezie Baker, for believing my tennis teachings should be in a book, for persuading me to begin, for her publicity instincts and continuing support.

To Mickey and Jim Cox for first suggesting I write a book at least 30 years ago when I worked in their sports shop, and for being faithful friends for over 50 years.

To my nephew Charles Crawford and his wife Sandy for reviewing early drafts of my manuscript and cheering me on.

To Fronia Corry for excellent editing and organizational suggestions, for having faith in the project, and for being a dear friend since high school days.

To Annette Harper, Sam and Nancy Roberts and Anna May Charrington for copyediting and thoughtful comments.

To Woody and Betsey Corkran for their photographic support - helping to see me portrayed in a good light.

To Annette Gow for her marketing know-how.

To my three sons, Paul, Jay and Mark, and three daughters-in-law, Mary, Carol and Jan, for their continuing encouragement, emotional support and love.

INTRODUCTION

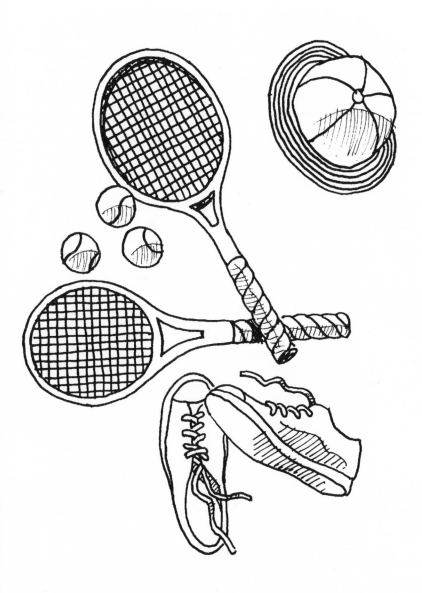

I have been involved in tennis for all but 13 years of my life and in coaching and teaching for 57 years. Now that I have retired, it is time to write down some of what I've learned and passed along to my students over the years, some of the tennis philosophy I have developed and the wisdom I have gained while involved in this terrifically interesting, wonderful sport.

I hope the ideas contained in these pages will help individuals to become well-rounded players, not just hard hitters. This is not a book outlining specific strokes or diagramming drills. It is about understanding the sport well enough to get out on the court and have a good time, using your mind to develop strategies that work for you, using your body to its best advantage at the level you wish to play.

Tennis is a sport for life. It's a sport for the beginner, the competitor, the social player, and the world class player; in other words, tennis is a sport that is ongoing at any age for a good healthy, active life. It's a game that you can begin at any age or stage in life. Perhaps you will improve enough to concentrate on tournament play for a period, while at another time you will simply want to play tennis as a social outlet. Many tennis players continue to enjoy this sport into their 80's and beyond.

In the interest of simplicity, I have chosen to use the pronoun "he" throughout the text when referring to another player. If you are a female, please read "she." I very much hope both sexes will find some helpful information in these chapters.

W. G.

TABLE OF CONTENTS

1. TENNIS: THE SPORT FOR LIFE

I have always tried to use clear and concise language in giving instructions to pupils, but there have been times when clear and concise wasn't enough. Sometimes the listener heard something I didn't know I had expressed. Once I had a pupil who had been born in England and, though we spoke the same language, it turned out she was not familiar with American colloquialisms. One day, during her lesson, I said to her, "Mary, back up." She looked puzzled and responded, "I beg your pardon?" So I repeated, "Mary, back up," at which point she walked up to the net and said to me, "Winnie, you're telling me to go in two directions at once."

Though occasionally I had to explain something more than once when instructing a pupil, verbal communication has been my stock in trade during my career. Verbal instruction and explanation along with an occasional demonstration have been the methods I've used to help a great many tennis players to improve and, so far, it's the only form of teaching I know. Now I am faced with a blank page and a new adventure in communicating, and I hope I'm up to the task.

Start with tennis. If you have the opportunity to learn tennis at an early age, take advantage of that opportunity. Tennis is undeniably the most difficult racquet sport because the mechanics of the game are, at once, subtle and complex and learning them can be demanding. It's hard to play tennis well without some help with your mechanics but if you learn tennis first, you can usually play any other racquet sport with facility.

Beginning tennis later in life will require dedication and patience but, fortunately, tennis has become an enormously popular game so you'll have no trouble finding willing players with whom to practice. After you become a confident tennis player, other racquet sports will not be too difficult to learn.

A lifetime sport. There are no short cuts to becoming a tennis player. You have to put in the time and the effort, but the reward is that you will be able to play this enjoyable and healthy sport for a lifetime. Once you leave high school or college, it is difficult to get eight other people to play softball or ten others to play hockey. Being involved in an individual sport allows you to participate for a lifetime.

Never too old. It's a myth that you cannot learn or improve in tennis after age 30. If you're a beginner at 30 or 35, there's no reason why you can't become a top level player by 35 or 40 if you're willing to practice. It's a matter of how hard you work and how much time you devote to physical and mental workouts on the court. Like anything else which requires practice and concentration, you get out of this game exactly what you put into it, nothing more, nothing less. Every time you go on the court, you have an opportunity to learn.

A racquet and some balls are the only equipment required to play this game. Combine that equipment with a willing spirit and you have all the tools necessary to become a first rate tennis player. What you do with those tools is up to you. You can build a fine game by learning how to use the racquet and move your feet. Every shot you make is, potentially, a new lesson: did the ball go where I wanted it to go? did I hit it deep enough? did I hit it solidly or off-center? When you're in the process of learning the game, you mustn't think of mishits or poor shots as errors, but as positive learning experiences, each shot a lesson in itself.

3

Know your priorities. To get the most enjoyment out of tennis, first establish your expectations and priorities. How proficient do you want to become? If you let the tennis court and your game become a source of stress, you will have no enjoyment at all. So you must decide your priorities and then be consistent with these priorities. Remember, however, that you will need to reevaluate these expectations periodically.

The years of raising young children, for instance, can be so consuming that there is little time to play tennis. Periods of job traveling or caring for an aging relative can become life priorities at different stages, when tennis must be relegated to the back burner. If you're at the stage in your life when tennis is the #4 priority, then that is what you must expect from yourself when you go on the court. If tennis is #4 and you go on the court expecting to play like it's #1, you will come off the court a mass of frustration and not enjoy the game at all. It's very important for your enjoyment of the game that you be consistent with your priorities. If tennis is #4, then expect #4 from yourself.

Set realistic goals for yourself. You have to understand who you are and where you are, not only in your expectations as to what level tennis player you wish to become, but where you are in a given match, on a given day. Being able realistically to evaluate your capabilities and your goals will allow you to play at that level and work to improve gradually. The greatest stumbling block to improvement is frustration, not a poor backhand, a poor forehand or a poor serve. Frustration begins with unrealistic goals. If you've set your goals too high, you'll never find enough practice time to reach those goals. People who set impossible goals are the ones who eventually give up the game.

Stay within your capabilities. To become a good tennis player, you must learn to stay within your capabilities, which means *never hitting the ball harder than you can control with consistency.* And your capabilities may be different every day, so you must be prepared to adjust your game each time you play. One day you can go on the court and hit the ball harder than you can on another day. Many players love to bang away at the ball, mistakenly assuming that power will produce the most points.

You have to learn quickly when you arrive on the court just what you are capable of that day. If you can do that, you will become a more consistent tennis player because you will learn to adjust to your present capabilities. Complete concentration is what you will need to analyze your effectiveness on a given day and to adjust your game to match that day's capabilities, reminding yourself *never to hit the ball harder than you can control with consistency.*

Practice good habits. To improve, it's important to have a commitment, a commitment to practice, to understanding the game and understanding there are no quick cures for problems. There are only two things you can practice: bad habits and good habits. If you practice bad habits, your game will decline. A good motto to remember is "Practice makes perfect if the practice is perfect."

Think constantly. Tennis is a head trip! You must deal with a great many mental intangibles which, if corralled and controlled, can make you a winning player: determination, drive, motivation and, the biggest intangible, confidence. If you are lacking in confidence, you're in deep trouble and you will defeat yourself. Mental acuity on the court is a practiced skill.

Learning to concentrate on one thing at a time, for instance how your opponent slices his backhand, will help you to anticipate well, then return that shot well, thereby building your confidence. Every player in the world can be a great player mentally. Club players will probably not reach the physical stature of the pros, but they can attain the pros' mental level. It's for that reason that, at 35 or older, you can continue to improve, even though your physical peak may have come and gone. You can still outthink other players.

Mind control. *You do on the tennis court what you think you can do.* To become a real tennis player rather than just a hitter, you must control your thoughts by concentrating on the right things: your own and your opponent's game plan. Everything you do on the court comes from intense concentration.

Challenge yourself. To continue to improve, you must have a purpose and a goal every time you step out onto the tennis court. And you must challenge yourself both physically and mentally because, just as a stroke needs drill and practice, your concentration also must be improved. Think at all times. Play every point with a purpose; don't just hit the ball aimlessly over the net. If you hone your concentration along with your playing skills, when the big point comes, you'll be ready.

6

What is percentage tennis? To be a "percentage player" you should use the shot, in every situation, that has the greatest chance of being successful. Hitting the ball is only the beginning of this game; keeping the ball in play one shot longer than your opponent can is what wins points and games. You want to play in such a way as to make the most of your strengths and minimize your weaknesses. Use the shot that will allow you to stay in the point or get back into the point if you're in trouble. If you have a great lob, use it when you're in trouble. If your overhead is weak, let the ball bounce before hitting it.

Keep the ball in play. The admonition "keep the ball in play" is so obvious, it has become a cliché. However, there is a simple explanation as to why this cliché must be your primary goal. A very high percentage of points are won or lost on *errors.* In fact, most points are scored on *unforced errors,* so if you can keep the ball in play long enough to *give your opponent a chance to make his percentage of errors*, you will prevail. Remember that the player who gets the ball over the net and into the court one more time than his opponent does will win the point.

Play it safe. Don't go for the big shot if you don't need to. You don't want to be the player who's making the biggest percentage of the errors, so use the shot that's the safest to keep the ball in play. You almost always have more than one shot to choose from and one of the choices generally has the better chance of success. As an example, if you are hitting from behind the baseline, the cross court shot is more likely to be successful than a down-the-line shot, since you will be hitting into the largest part of the court over the lowest part of the net. Best to play it safe on most points, and let your opponent make the errors.

The list of excuses for playing poorly seems endless and in 57 years of teaching and coaching, I suppose I've heard most of them. "I drank too much water, the strings were too loose, I needed new balls, I played too late, I played too early." One of my all-time favorites, probably the quintessential excuse, was "My bracelets were too heavy." When playing with friends for fun or competitively, there is nothing worse than spoiling your opponent's win with endless excuses. It's poor sportsmanship and just plain tacky.

Eliminate your excuses. Excuses are for losers and, indeed, make you more likely to lose. Excuse-givers squander their mental energy by looking backward at useless problems rather than focusing their energy on the job at hand. The excuse-maker is concerned with explaining why he is losing or has lost and, in any case, his excuses are seldom factual. The winning player, on the other hand, is concerned with doing what it takes to play well during a match.

2. THE BASICS

A t this point in my life, after so many years of teaching, I realize the most interesting people I taught were those who had played for a number of years and were ready to move to the next level, or simply to improve on what they had been doing. I believe these pupils often sought me out for lessons because they knew that I wouldn't try to "break down" their game.

If a player is comfortable with his grip and has some "tried and true" shots, it's best to build on that foundation. If a player has a terrible grip but can still produce good shots, I recommend against changing the grip. There's always some infinitesimal thing in a player's game that, if properly diagnosed and changed or rearranged, can give that player instant improvement. If you break down a player's basic strokes or grips and try to instruct him from scratch, it takes at least six weeks for him to begin to see positive results from the changes. Most seasoned players have neither the time nor inclination to put up with a 6-week period of relearning. At that stage of a player's tennis life, starting over is very discouraging.

Check out the pro. If you decide you need a pro to help you or your child with some basic strokes, do lots of chatting with friends who play or whose children play tennis. You might try checking with your local tennis association for names of several pros within your area. Many people don't bother to check, but it's important that you do. Before you turn yourself or your child over to a teacher instructor, you should have, at least, some word-of-mouth knowledge of his background.

Some pros today are just drillmasters - they simply want to run drills. They get out on the court with a machine and have the students hit balls as hard as they can hit them, 400 times, with nothing in mind, no idea where to direct the ball. Many of these students are "long on the racquet" - a term which means the heel of the hand is beyond the end of the racquet handle. This is one of the most significant reasons for the development of tennis elbow. (Refer to *Tennis Elbow* in Chapter 11.)

Start with the laces: The laces in all athletic shoes, including tennis shoes, should be *inverted* in the top holes on either side; in other words, the *top holes only* should be laced from the outside inward. This allows you to tie the shoe tighter, which gives you better support for the ankle. At the same time, the lace will not be as inclined to loosen, as it does when it is laced in the conventional way and then pulled very tightly. Shoes tied with the top laces inverted will stay tightly tied throughout even the most grueling match.

With the quick stops in the game of tennis, many players find that their feet slide forward in their shoes and their big

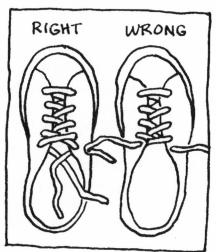

toe hits the front of their sneaker. This can cause pain and a condition known as "tennis toe." If you lace your sneaker with the top lace going from the outside inward, this will keep your foot from sliding forward on your quick stops, thereby eliminating the "tennis toe" problem.

11

In addition to tennis players, other athletes would benefit from learning this method of shoe lacing; nurses and others in occupations which require that they be on their feet all day would do well to tie that top lace from the outside in.

Two part tennis: Tennis is divided into two parts: racquet work and footwork, and the percentage of each is not 50/50.

<u>*About 75-80% of tennis is footwork.*</u>
Why is it that when we make an error we glare accusingly at our racquet as if it were the culprit when, in fact, more often than not, it is our feet which have caused the error? It's very difficult to hit the ball well when you are not in good position. You can't expect your racquet to do what your feet need to do.

When I began to coach wheelchair players, I decided I had better get into the wheelchair myself to figure out just what they were going to have to cope with. It was a great source of astonishment to me to learn that a wheelchair player hits the ball virtually the same as does a stand-up player.

The secret is to get the wheelchair *into good position* just as a stand-up player must be in good position before hitting the ball. You simply cannot hit the ball well if you're not in the proper position, in or out of the chair. Your racquet cannot do what your feet or chair have to do. Tennis, remember, is about 75% footwork and 25% racquet work, not 50% of each.

Play with energy. Keep your feet moving all the time, side to side, up and back. Take deep breaths through your nose and exhale through your mouth. This will help to eliminate let-downs and keep up your energy level.

Speed, pace and spin: Tennis balls are hit with speed, pace and spin. The more *spin,* the less *speed.* Putting spin on the ball can be accomplished in three ways: top spin, slice (or chop) and side spin.

1) Top spin is produced by starting with the racquet below the ball and finishing your stroke above the ball.

2) A slice is produced by starting with the racquet above the ball and finishing the stroke with the racquet below the ball.

3) Side spin is produced by hitting across the ball.

You will want all of these shots in your arsenal, so practice each separately to see how each works for you and to discover which shot you can use in which circumstances.

Changing the speed and spin you put on each ball is more effective than always hitting with the same speed and spin. It breaks up your opponent's timing and doesn't allow him to get into a groove.

Footwork produces pace. It's important for players to know the difference between *speed* and *pace* on a ball. *Speed* is how fast the ball is traveling and is generated totally by how fast the racquet head comes through when it is making contact with the ball. *Pace* is a combination of ball speed and body weight, and is totally generated by proper footwork.

To get *pace* on the ball, you must get your body weight into the shot. It is preferable to hit the ball with *pace* for this reason: with your body weight behind the ball, you don't have to hit the ball as hard and, therefore, you will have better control and greater consistency. When a player says his opponent is hitting a "heavy ball," this is a reference to a ball which has been hit with *pace*.

"HEAVY BALL"

Step in. "Stepping into the ball" means stepping straight towards the net. When your racquet is back, your weight is back and, as your racquet comes forward, your weight comes forward onto the front foot, stepping into the shot (and producing *pace* on the ball).

Imagine a line drawn perpendicular to the net all the way to the baseline. Both toes should be touching that imaginary line when you are about to hit a ball. It is important, however, *that the front foot be at a 45° angle to the net while the back foot is parallel to the net.* If, instead, your front foot is parallel to the net, your weight won't move through the stroke because your ankle bone simply doesn't bend in that direction and will not allow your weight to come through.

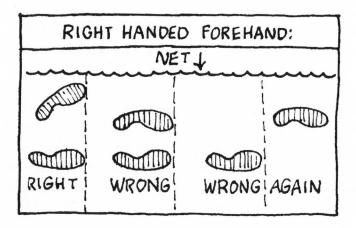

That last step before hitting the ball should be a small one. You will naturally begin with your weight back when your racquet is back. As you bring your racquet forward, your weight will come with it, going right into the shot. That produces *pace*.

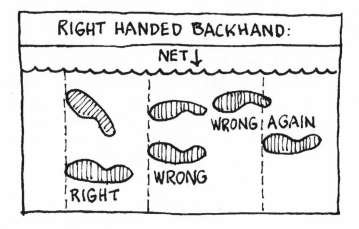

One extra piece of advice: as you follow through on the shot, the right heel of the back foot should lift off the court and turn out for balance, but the entire foot should not leave the court, only the heel.

Shuffle for positioning. To move sideways, the shuffle step is extremely important (sliding your feet from side to side on the court, as opposed to moving forward and back). Learn to use it. From the shuffle step, it is a natural movement to step forward, into the ball. As long as you have time to get to the ball, the shuffle step is the correct way to move around the court from side to side. It is a vital part of your footwork and it will put you in position to *step into the ball* properly as you hit it. When you use the shuffle step, the natural thing to do with the last step is to go forward toward the net. The correct footwork, at this point, is to *bring your toes into line with each other* (touching that imaginary perpendicular line pictured on page 15).

Open or Closed. Of course there will be times when, to get to the ball in time, you will have to abandon the shuffle step, crossing your feet over one another as you go wide for a tough shot. On the backhand, this dash to reach the ball often will result in the last step being taken by the foot nearest the net, with the other foot behind, which will produce a "closed stance." With your feet in this position, you cannot step into the ball, meaning toward the net, as your feet are now headed for the side line and you cannot shift your weight into the shot. With this "closed stance," you will have only the power of your arm behind your shot, putting no *pace* on the ball, only *speed*. When hitting a defensive shot such as this, do your best to hit deep.

On the forehand, a more prevalent mistake is for players to hit with an "open stance," with the player essentially facing the net. You can't shift your weight forward with an open stance either. Therefore, you'll be hitting the shot entirely with your arm, with no body weight coming into the shot (and no *pace* on the ball). This produces nothing but *speed*, not nearly as effective as a ball with *pace*.

Pace cannot be attained with either a closed backhand stance or an open forehand stance. Only correct foot positioning will produce a ball hit with *pace*.

FOREHAND

CORRECT STANCE   OPEN STANCE

Place the ball through timing. Timing where your racquet meets the ball is a crucial element of learning to be a good player. This is called "placing the ball through timing." If your footwork is correct, to place the ball through timing means meeting the ball in different positions in relation to your body.

Let's assume you are a right handed player hitting a forehand.

   a. If you want to hit the ball crosscourt, you must meet the ball *a little bit in front of your left, or front, foot.*

   b. If you want to hit the ball right down the middle of the court, you must meet the ball *directly opposite your left, or front, foot.*

   c. And if you want to hit the ball down the line, you must meet the ball *opposite your left, or front, heel.*

If you don't meet each of these balls at the correct point in relationship to your feet, the shot won't go where you expect it to go.

"Placing the ball through timing" has nothing to do with changing your footwork, rather it requires that your footwork be correct and consistent, and that you be accurate in your timing, connecting with each ball at the proper moment.

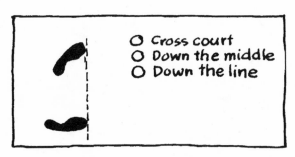

It is equally as crucial to "place the ball through timing" for your backhand shots, keeping in mind that the backhand shots differ slightly from the forehand. With all three backhand shots (crosscourt, down the middle and down the line) the ball must be met a little earlier in relationship to your body.

Learning to "place the ball through timing" will give you two distinct advantages over your opponent. First, you can disguise your shots very well. With consistent footwork and such a small differential between where you meet each ball, there is no way anyone can tell ahead of time where the ball will be placed. Second, planning your timing for when you are going to meet the ball is the only concrete, physical way to ensure that you watch the ball all the way to the racquet face.

Backswing in motion. If you start your backswing when your opponent's ball crosses the net and time your backswing to move at the same speed as the ball which is headed your way, this will give you an unbroken, unhurried swing, the kind all good players have and the rest of us strive for.

Squeeze: When you start your backswing and throughout your whole stroke, you should squeeze the handle of the racquet. For the forehand shot, you should feel pressure on the first knuckle of the thumb and that will tighten up your wrist for the forehand shot. If you are having trouble with a floppy wrist, putting pressure on the first knuckle of the thumb will automatically tighten up your wrist.

When the stroke is finished, you must release your grip in order to be able to change your grip for another shot. So the rhythm is: squeeze, release, squeeze, release. If you squeeze when you hit each shot, you will hear a nice popping sound as the racquet hits the ball. If you forget to squeeze, your shots will sound slushy, with no pop. When playing against a hard hitter, connecting with the ball can knock the face of your racquet back unless you are squeezing on each shot.

Limits on your strokes: We all strive to acquire perfect strokes. The impression seems to be that if we can learn these idyllic strokes, whatever they are, we will be victorious in our play. But even if you manage to develop beautiful strokes, you will still be constrained by the limitations of their use.

Remember, you must be in a perfect position to hit a perfect stroke which, most of the time, you are not. So instead of worrying about perfection in your form, learn to adjust your strokes, changing speed or using spins, and learn to win points without perfect strokes.

Consistency, accuracy, variety. At every level of tennis, errors outnumber winning placements by a large percentage. As you practice your shots, you should work on *consistency* first, making sure your shots consistently go over the net and into the court. Recognize that your greatest enemy is the net, not your opponent.

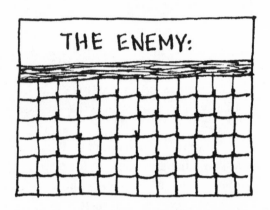

Later, you will want to work on fine tuning your shots with *accuracy*, trying to keep your shots as deep as possible in the opponent's court.

Finally, you should try to develop some *variety* in your shot-making, working on speed and spins and disguise.

Of course, this all takes time, but if you practice your basic strokes in this order, working on *consistency, then accuracy, then variety,* you will be less likely to make errors. Eventually you may want to hit with more power, but this is the last element of your game to work on.

If you've mastered *consistency, accuracy and variety*, you needn't worry about power, because before you get an opportunity to hit the big shot, you will have won the point.

Where's the big shot? It's a tennis myth that you need a lot of "big shots" in your game to be a winner. In singles, if you get the ball over the net after the serve 2 and 2/10 times, you'll win about 75% of the points. In doubles, if you get the the ball over the net after the serve 4 and 4/10 times, you'll win about 75% of the points. You don't need big shots to do this; you need consistency. Just get the ball over the net.

One shot longer. Attempting to hit the ball above your capabilities will result in loss of control and consistency. Remember that you should be aware of your capabilities, in general and on a given day, and should play within that boundary in order to stay in control. To repeat: the secret is to keep the ball in the court one shot longer than your opponent does.

Position yourself. Players limit their ability to hit good strokes by late preparation and poor positioning. It's very, very difficult to hit the ball well when you're not in the proper position. If you're not fully prepared when the opponent's ball reaches you, you should hit a defensive shot, and hit it as deep as possible into his court.

Build in some leeway. Trying to place the ball too close to the lines or too close to the top of the net is unwise. You must leave some margin for error. Playing a ball too close to the lines will result in the most errors, although skimming the net is also very hazardous. Plan to clear the net by the length of a tennis racquet. If you plan to clear the net by 2", your ball will wind up about halfway down the net. If you give yourself some leeway, planning mentally to clear the tape by the height of a racquet, you'll hit far fewer balls into the net.

Leave margin for error. The closest that you should mentally plan to hit to an outside line is about the width of the alley. But, if you're going to change the direction of the ball by, for example, returning a crosscourt shot down the line, you have to give yourself even more margin for error or you will likely hit the ball wide. So, when changing the direction of the ball, you should mentally increase that alley width by about one-half so as not to hit wide; that is, mentally, an alley and a half when changing direction.

Use the volley. Aggressive tennis means moving forward. In doubles, you should be trying to take the net, so the volley is very important. There are three areas for a volley: Volley 1 is used when the ball approaches you anywhere from the chest up, Volley 2 is used when the ball comes at you between chest level and the middle of the thigh, and Volley 3 is used when the ball level is from the mid-thigh downward. Your racquet should stay in the same volley plane all the way through the stroke. The difference will be in your body position, whether you are reaching up for the easier Volley 1 or bending your knees to get below the net for the more difficult Volley 3.

Racquet face above the wrist. Every volley should be hit with the racquet head above your wrist, no matter what the ball height, and *the volley should be hit with slice and not top spin.* To produce a slice, the swing should begin above the ball and finish below the ball.

The volley is about a 12" shot from beginning to end. Volleys should be hit without a backswing so the 12" range is all moving forward. You should meet the ball in front of you, but not too far in front, as you want to still be able to move your racquet forward after the ball makes contact. To meet the ball correctly, the butt of the racquet should point to the heel of the front foot. If executed correctly, you will be able to have about a 12" follow through. Also, if the butt of the racquet is pointing to the front heel, the racquet head will have to be above the wrist, as is proper.

Approach Shot. An approach shot means that you approach the net after you have returned the ball to your opponent. An approach shot is only hit off of a short ball - one that lands well inside the baseline. It's not a good idea to try to approach the net following a shot that has been hit very deep into your court.

It's very important that you hit your approach *deep*, and it should be hit *straight ahead* from your particular position on the court. If you are on the right side of the center service line, you should hit the ball straight ahead to the left hand side of your opponent's court. If the ball arrives on your side of the net near the center service line, you should return it straight down that center line. If the ball lands on the left hand side of your court, you want to return it straight to the right hand side of your opponent's court.

All of this is to cut down on the angles which your opponent will be able to return to you. If you hit the ball deep and straight, you will be well positioned to intercept the return with a volley; you will have given yourself a better chance for court coverage, while giving your opponent less chance to hit a good angle shot.

If, however, you expect to make a winner with your approach shot, then you are not restricted to hitting straight ahead because you don't expect the ball to come back; the point will be over.

Drop Shot. A drop shot is a ball which lands very close to the net. It is a very effective tennis shot. Like the approach shot, the drop shot should be hit off of a ball that lands well inside the baseline. If you try to hit a drop shot from the baseline, the ball will take such a long time to get over the net that your opponent will have plenty of time to run it down.

A drop shot should have underspin (slice) on it because the ball with underspin does not travel as far toward the opponent after it bounces, so there is less time to retrieve it.

In most cases, the best percentage play for the drop shot is to hit it cross court. You'll be hitting it over the lowest part of the net (the center where the net dips) and hitting away from the opponent, so he'll have a greater distance to cover to get to the ball.

It's a good idea to couple the drop shot with a lob. Once you have your opponent racing up to the net to retrieve your drop shot, lob over his head to win the point.

The Overhead. An overhead is almost always hit with the ball up in the air and your racquet above your head, before the ball bounces. However, if the ball is very deep and you have to go to the baseline to hit it, it's sometimes better to let the ball bounce and then hit it at the top of its flight. This ball can still be hit as an overhead.

You should keep your overhead shot far enough in front of you so that you have to step into the ball to hit it. The difference between an overhead and a serve is this: with the serve your racquet goes down along the side of your leg before it goes up to make contact with the ball. With an overhead, you lift your racquet right up with no preliminary dropping motion.

When you hit an overhead, have a spot it mind for which you are aiming. A crosscourt shot will generally give you more room and the greatest margin for error. Whether you hit crosscourt or not, always try to hit to the open court.

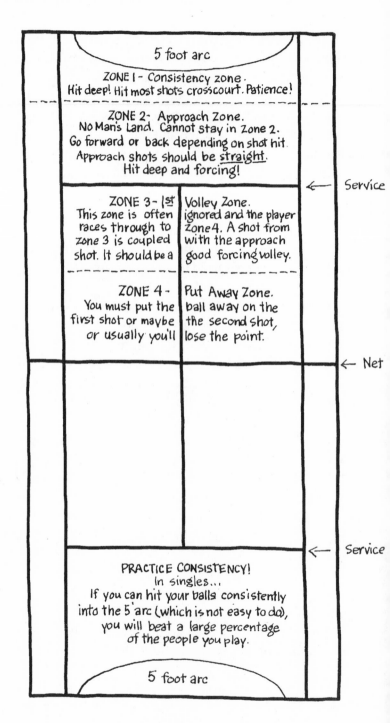

5 foot arc

ZONE 1 - Consistency zone.
Hit deep! Hit most shots crosscourt. Patience!

ZONE 2- Approach Zone.
No Man's Land. Cannot stay in Zone 2.
Go forward or back depending on shot hit.
Approach shots should be straight.
Hit deep and forcing!

← Service

ZONE 3 - 1st | Volley Zone.
This zone is often | ignored and the player
races through to | Zone 4. A shot from
zone 3 is coupled | with the approach
shot. It should be a | good forcing volley.

ZONE 4 - | Put Away Zone.
You must put the | ball away on the
first shot or maybe | the second shot,
or usually you'll | lose the point.

← Net

← Service

PRACTICE CONSISTENCY!
In singles...
If you can hit your balls consistently
into the 5' arc (which is not easy to do),
you will beat a large percentage
of the people you play.

5 foot arc

The Lob. The lob is a ball hit high into the air in a looping arc. When your opponent pushes you behind your baseline, your best percentage shot is to hit a high, deep lob crosscourt. You are less likely to make an error with a lob than with any other shot.

An *offensive* lob is used when you arc the ball over your opponent who has approached the net, high enough so that he can't reach it but not so high as to allow him to retreat and retrieve it at the baseline.

A *defensive* lob is used if you have been pulled out of position. Even if your opponent is at the baseline, a lob will give you more time to regroup and get back into the proper position.

Anticipation is not guesswork; it is *analysis*.

Following are some things that you can do
to improve your anticipation.

See the racquet. When you hit the ball to your opponent, your attention is on the ball. But as soon as your opponent begins his backswing, you need to switch your attention from the ball to your opponent's racquet face. If you put your whole attention on the opponent's racquet face as soon as he starts his backswing, you will improve your anticipation and start to get into position sooner to receive his shot earlier.

Seeing your opponent's racquet head should be as automatic as breathing. You will still visually follow the ball as it goes right to your opponent's racquet, but your whole attention is now on the racquet *head*. It will not tell you where your opponent is going to hit the ball, but *it will tell you what kind of speed and what kind of spin the ball will have.*

For instance, the faster the racquet comes through, the more speed will be on the ball. If your opponent hits *up* on the ball, the ball will have top spin, and a top spin ball, after it bounces, will travel much farther towards you than if it had been hit with slice or underspin.

If your opponent's racquet chops at the ball in a downward motion, from above to below the ball, that ball has been sliced. To respond to a slice, you need to "open" your racquet face for your return. This means to tilt the racquet slightly so the face is pointing upwards, not perpendicular to the court. Without this adjustment, you will likely return a slice into the net.

A slice may also be returned with a top spin shot, but whichever shot you choose, open your racquet face slightly if you're returning a slice to avoid hitting into the net.

Practice transferring your focus to your opponent's racquet until it becomes automatic. You will be amazed how much sooner you will get started for the ball and how you will be able to reach balls you never got to before. If you don't see your opponent's racquet face, you won't know how the ball has been hit until after it bounces on your side of the net, and that makes you a week late and a dollar short.

Watch the player. Not only is it important to see your opponent's racquet head but also to see his feet and body position. Very often, when you note how his feet are set up, you will be better able to anticipate where he will place his shot.

Follow the ball. In doubles, when a ball is hit to your partner, an important way to improve your anticipation is to visually follow the ball back to your partner's racquet. If you see your partner hit the ball, you will know where his ball is going to go so you can plan earlier.

If your partner hits a short lob, short enough for the opponent at the net to reach it, you need to move back as soon as the ball leaves your partner's racquet. If you have not turned your head and taken a look at your partner, you won't know what his ball is going to do until it crosses in front of you, and that's much too late. It can also be dangerous. You need to know ahead of time if you need to get out of there, to retreat from the net.

Be sure, however, when you are checking to see your partner hit the ball that this is not a long look - not a stare. And don't turn your back to your opponents. This look to check your partner's racquet is simply a quick back and forth glance. You need to still be aware of what is going on on the other side of the net. Throughout the game it is necessary to turn your head back and forth constantly, seeing both sides of the net, checking how your partner is hitting the ball as well as what your opponents are doing.

Here is another example of how our words can be misunderstood.

At one time I taught a young boy of about nine years old who had had a stroke when he was seven. He had some paralysis in his right leg and had lost the use of his right, dominant hand so I started teaching him to play with his left hand. He did very well, improving rapidly, and in one lesson I said to him, "Now's the time for me to teach you something about anticipation. You're hitting the ball very well but we need to get you started sooner so you can get to more balls." So we talked in that lesson all about anticipation.

The next morning his mother called me on the phone and said, "I just had to call you! When Brad got into the car after his lesson yesterday, he said, 'That was a wonderful lesson. I loved it and I learned all there is to learn about constipation.'"

3. PRACTICE

hy am I here? You have to know before you go on the court why you're going out there. Are you out there to practice or on the court to score? In each of these instances, you must think about entirely different things. When you are on the court to compete or score, you must never think about your mechanics. When you're on the court to improve your game, which is to practice, that's when you should concentrate on your mechanics and not worry about the score.

Practice with a purpose. Your method of practice is very important. If you try just these two suggestions, you will be amazed at your improved play.

1. Practice with a purpose, and that means having a plan for every ball you hit.

2. Take every ball on the first bounce. Unless you're a wheel chair player, you won't ever play a regular game with two bounces. Make yourself move, be there!

Prepare to win. Everyone goes on the court wanting to win. We all have the will to win, but not everyone has the will *to prepare* to win. Remember the motto: "Practice makes perfect if the practice is perfect." Practicing with a purpose will produce good habits and improve your play. Aimless practice produces aimless play; mindful practice produces mindful play. Good practice habits will result in much improved performance both in competitive and social tennis. And, of course, the better we play, the more we enjoy any sport.

Play all levels. It's a tennis myth that the only way to improve is to play better players. Not so. To improve your tennis game, you should choose opponents of all abilities. You should play with those better than you, those of equal ability, and those of lesser ability. Of these categories, you will actually have the best practice sessions with the players of lesser ability.

Call a weaker player. Contrary to popular belief, your best practice will be with someone of lesser ability than yourself. Practicing with a weaker player allows you to concentrate entirely on your mechanics.

When you play with someone who is not as good, you are accomplishing two things: first, you are investing an hour in another human being. There is nothing that makes a tennis player feel better than to have a superior player call him and say, "Hey, would you like to hit some balls?"

Second, when practicing with a weaker player, you can devise a strategy that includes helping him while helping yourself. Always play to his strength so, for your sake, the ball is more than likely to come back and, for his sake, he will be grooving a shot he can rely on.

To make the practice especially worthwhile, pick out a weakness in your own game and work on that weakness as much as possible. If you want to improve your mid-court volley, get yourself to mid-court as often as possible to practice that shot. This kind of practice will be your best bet for improving your weaker strokes.

The best and the brightest. If you *always* play with a superior tennis player, most of the time you will walk out on the court thinking "I hope I can give him a good game."

For similar reasons, you should not *always* choose to play with someone of equal ability if you wish to practice and improve your game, because you will go out on the court thinking you should beat him. Neither one of these thought processes will help you to have a good practice session since you'll be trying to score points and won't, therefore, practice your weaker strokes and shots.

You will, however, learn other things by practicing with equal or superior players, so this practice can be worthwhile also. If you are losing to the player with equal or greater ability, you will learn about concentration and how to "hang in there," knowing you always have a chance.

Be enthusiastic. You can improve faster by practicing hard for one hour than by going through the motions for three hours. Once you lose your enthusiasm during your practice, it's better to just stop and get off the court.

Warm up slowly. When you first go on the court, you should begin warming up by hitting the ball quite easily; that way you will get a lot of balls in and you'll be inclined to think "Oh, I'm hitting the ball pretty well today." If you begin your warm-up by hitting the ball as hard as you can, you will spray the balls all over the place and make a ton of errors and you'll begin to think, "Oh, I'm not going to be able to hit anything in today."

Groove your strokes. During the warm-up, you want to hit the ball directly to your opponent. The purpose of the warm-up is not to make winners. You want to hit the ball back to your opponent so you both can hit as many balls as possible. That way you will "warm up" not only your muscles but your strokes, which is exactly what you need to do before playing.

Play games. Even though you are out on the court to practice, you should get into a playing situation after you warm up. You should not continually hit the ball back and forth as you do in the warm-up session, but eventually should begin to play games, keeping score as in a match, though not concentrating on the score, not worrying about winning or losing. You will have a good practice session if you concentrate on your mechanics.

4. CONCENTRATION

C oncentration is disciplining yourself to eliminate any thoughts that creep into your mind except the proper ones, those which pertain to the task at hand, as well as understanding your own capabilities in a given situation. Every aspect of *becoming a good tennis player demands intense concentration.*

A thinking game. Tennis is a very complex game and the most intellectual of all active sports. Perhaps you cannot hit like the pros, but you can learn to think like them. Stamina, style and perfect strokes are of no avail if you don't think about *strategy, tactics, and what your opponent is doing.*

In a competition between opponents of equal ability, the winner in most matches will be the player who knows the strokes, the style, and the psychology of his opponent and who hits every ball with a purpose. At the conclusion of a competitive match, you should come off the court as mentally tired as you are physically, *if* you have been thinking about the proper things throughout the whole match.

I suppose that's the reason I get bent out of shape when I think someone's playing brain dead tennis. I never can remember hitting a tennis ball without a purpose. I always knew what I wanted to do with the ball. I always had something in mind.

Tennis is so much more enjoyable when you're using your head. Planning how to play each point, plus how and where to hit each shot, will increase your level of concentration, improving your game each time you play. What could be more fun than that?

Stay in control. *The best hit tennis ball in the whole world is worth only one point. The worst hit tennis ball in the whole world is worth only one point.* So don't get too elated or too despondent over either shot, not too *up* over the good shot or too *down* over the bad. It's vital that you stay in control. Lose control of yourself and you will lose control of your game.

Eliminate mindless hitting. Always have in mind a place where you want to hit the ball. This is true of groundstrokes, volleys and serves. If you have no spot in mind, you cannot learn from your own errors. Try always to make the correct shot choice, which is the one with the best chance of success, not the one where you are likely to make an error.

Most players know the safer or better percentage shot to use, but many just can't resist hitting the "ego" shot. You may get away with the ego shot now and then but, over the long haul, you're better off with the safe shot. The "percentage" shot will help you score better in a competitive situation. Even in a practice match you will keep the ball in play longer.

Watch the ball longer. If you are on the court and not playing well, it is usually because you are not watching the ball *long enough*. In these circumstances, just telling yourself to "watch the ball" may not be enough to correct the situation because you *think* that you *are* watching the ball. The solution, therefore, is to watch the ball *longer,* all the way to the strings of your racquet until the ball makes contact. If you can force yourself to make this one change when you aren't playing well, your game will improve immediately.

Off-center hits are caused by not watching the ball *long enough*, nothing else. When the racquet torques in your hand, it happens because you have not watched the ball all the way to the strings and you connect off-center.

What's going on around you? In order to become a good tennis player, you must "get out of yourself." You must know more than just what you are doing; you must know what your opponents are doing and, if you are playing doubles, you must know what your partner is doing.

Doubles is like chess. What you do depends on what the other people on the court are doing. You are all interwoven and your next move is dictated by what your opponents and your partner did just moments before.

In club doubles, there are many pairs who don't try to come to the net. Some of them will position themselves one up and one back, or some prefer to play with both players back near the baseline.

What is your partner doing? Are you playing side by side, one up and one back or both back? All these positioning factors are vital to the decisions you make about your next shot, or how to win the point.

You have to be aware of what everyone is doing on the court so that you can make some intelligent plans.

Don't quit on yourself. In any competitive sport, there must be a winner and a loser. It's no fun to lose in an individual sport when you alone are responsible for the loss. But if you have played your best and not quit on yourself, there's no reason to be upset over losing a match. If you concentrated well, you undoubtedly learned something while on the court, perhaps something that will help you to win the next time.

On the other hand, if you quit on yourself and did not give the match your total attention, you *should* be upset with yourself.

Body language. On the tennis court, you often hear the comments of disgust over the bad shots: "Oh, how could I hit such a lousy shot!!?" You very, very seldom hear anyone express real pleasure with his own good shot, like: "Hey, baby, that was a super shot!"

Making a good shot will give you a lift, of course, but don't dwell on it. Move on. Stay in control. Try not to despair over the bad shots. Think ahead, not back. If you are disappointed in your game, don't let your body language show it. If your opponent recognizes that you are discouraged, he will likely take advantage of your let-down. *Make* him beat you, don't *help* him.

Shoe on the other foot. When your opponent has lost a couple of points, watch for the body language signals that indicate he is thinking about the wrong stuff and has lost the concentration necessary to play well. That's a good chance for some easy points. The obvious signals are displays of anger which include slouching around the court and talking to himself, either aloud or under his breath.

Be alert also to the less obvious body language which indicates a let-down, including a hang-dog look, less energetic and aggressive play, and a generally sluggish demeanor. Use this opportunity to be more aggressive yourself to capture a couple of quick points or games.

5. ETIQUETTE

A *traditional sport.* Tennis is filled with a great many traditions which should be observed. Perhaps the most important is always to give your opponent the benefit of the doubt on close decisions. The game should be played with sportsmanship, a minimal display of negativism, and no alibis. If you lose control of yourself, you will lose control of your game. "Losing it" is a luxury you cannot afford if you are to be a winning player, and a display of bad temper won't make you the most popular player at the club.

Be on time. Whether it be for competition or social play, don't arrive late! The quickest way to antagonize people is to make them wait for you. Your smooth apologies mean little.

Everyone's time is valuable. Your fellow players have set aside some of their precious time for a match and anticipated fun, while it appears that the latecomer is saying, "my time is more valuable than yours." Friends will understand the occasional emergency, but to be chronically late is inexcusable. Making people stand around and wait is very poor form. The best idea is to be ten minutes early, not ten minutes late.

Hit some serves. Practice all the serves you want. You need to loosen up your arm and shoulder and get the feel of your serve. You should practice until you produce a good serve. For this reason, you don't want to tell your opponent "I'll take a couple." It's possible you might want to hit six rather than two. Just inform your opponent, "This is practice." Once you feel you have control of your serve, you should announce that you are ready to begin.

First ball back. There should be no such thing as "First serve in," even in social tennis. It is against the rules. After warming up, when every player has had a chance to practice his serve, play begins.

First Serve In is very common in social tennis, but remember, First Serve In gives an enormous advantage to the server, allowing him to try spins or hard or soft serves, whatever suits his fancy, with no penalty if the serves all go out or into the net. In the meantime, the receiver is at a tremendous disadvantage since he is expected to hit whichever of these balls lands in the service court. My answer to "First serve in" is "Okay, first ball back." That way, the playing field is leveled, so to speak.

Calling the shots. Always make good calls. Even though it's often difficult to call the ball when you're running and reaching and your head is bouncing around, you must make your own calls and it's important to be decisive. Stalling is unacceptable. Make your calls quickly and fairly. If you are not sure, the call should *always* be decided in favor of your opponent.

Calling the score. It's always a good idea to call the score between points, being sure that everyone on the court can hear. Any player may do this, though the server is traditionally the one to make the announcement. If there is a disagreement about the score, all points should be verbally reconstructed. The score will revert to the point which all players can agree upon, even if the game has to begin again.

At the end of each game, it's also a good idea to announce the game score. The person who has just served is often the one to do this, though it is perfectly all right for anyone to call the game score. Just be sure the score is heard by every player on the court.

Nice people win. Make no mistake, nice people win. If you make a bad call and do not correct yourself, it will be on your mind for the rest of the match. That call was only worth one point, but you will have lost your self respect in the bargain and it's hard to do your best under these conditions. The players with whom you enjoy playing the most are the ones who observe the unwritten rules and traditions of the game.

Call 'em as you see 'em. In doubles, you and your partner should decide together who will call the serves. If your partner is more comfortable for you to call the serve that he is receiving, then do so. However, if your partner calls *any* ball "out," a serve or otherwise, when you have seen it as "good," you must, without question, overcall him and give the point to your opponents.

Give the benefit of the doubt. If you're not sure whether your opponent's ball is in or out when it lands on your side of the net, you must always give him the benefit of the doubt and call the ball "good." You don't ever play the point over by saying "I don't know whether it was in or out, so let's play a let." If you feel that your opponent had a better look at the ball, it is perfectly all right to ask whether he thought it was in or out, accepting his decision when he makes the call.

Conversely, you must not call a ball that you have hit when it lands on your opponent's side of the net. That call is his alone unless he asks for your help. If your opponent does ask, and you are sure that you saw how the ball landed, you don't want to say "Well, it's your call." Rather, you should call it as you saw it and he is obligated to accept your call.

Assume good faith. Don't get bent out of shape on calls of a half inch or less if you think they are miscalled. It is very difficult to know whether a ball is in or out from across the net and, in most cases, you should assume that your opponent, who is making his calls from close range, is trying to call the shots fairly. Most people are not cheaters; they're hopers. If you worry about what you perceive to be a miscall, you'll inevitably miss the next shot.

Of course, if your opponent is making miscalls that are very obviously in his favor, perhaps of an inch or more, that's another story. You have a right to be peeved. As a general rule, you are better off to stay out of any dispute about line calls, although, if the miscalls seem blatant, you might try asking, "Are you sure?" to let him know that you have some doubt about his eyesight. Intentional bad calls seldom happen, however. Nice people play tennis.

Always play it straight. What if the opponent cheats? Cheating is very rare in the sport of tennis, but what if you find yourself in a match where the opponent is the exception to the rule? It will do you no good to try to get even by imitating the behavior of a poor sport. Your ethics and code of behavior are extremely important, not to be altered by someone on the other side of the net. The real test of sportsmanship is how you act when someone else behaves badly. *You* play it straight.

Don't be a hypocrite. "I don't mind losing" is usually a bunch of baloney. Everybody wants to win. A good sport wants to win and hates to lose just as much as a bad sport does, but a good sport is careful not to display his anxiety or disappointment. And it's a fact that when a person controls himself, he controls his game, just the way that losing control of himself will cause his game to come apart.

There's no worse faux pas than for one of the players of a match to grumble as he is leaving the court, "Oh, I played terribly." All that does is spoil someone else's win and gives no credit to the grumbler's opponent. After all, that opponent might have had something to do with causing the grumbler to play badly.

Give credit where credit is due. It is poor taste to look bored when your opponent serves you an ace. There is nothing worse than calculated rudeness. Make your praise brief; you needn't give a speech to be a good sport, but give credit where credit is due. And avoid sarcasm, such as saying "Great shot" when your opponent makes a winner off the handle.

Common Courtesies. Wait, don't walk behind someone else's court while a point is in progress. Don't ask players on another court to return your ball while they're in the middle of a point, but pay attention to where your ball rolls so that if it goes behind another court and those players don't see it, you may ask for it at the appropriate time.

Call your own "let," not others'. If your ball rolls onto an adjacent court, never call a "let" for the players on that court. It is their responsibility to call the "let" if they are distracted by the rolling ball and wish play to be discontinued.

On the other hand, you may call a "let" anytime a loose ball runs onto your own court and, in fact, should call it immediately. If a ball is behind your opponent, you should call a "let" even if your opponent doesn't see it. It's vital to keep your court clear of loose balls. If you've ever seen a player step on a tennis ball, you'll understand why. It's not pretty!

If a "let" is called during a point, the server begins the point over again and always gets two serves, not just one.

Return precisely. Return balls to the server by hitting them directly to him; never just smack them randomly over the net. Check to see, or ask, if the server has two balls. Wait until the server turns to face you and is prepared to receive the ball, then hit the ball to him as accurately as you can so he may remain in position to serve and does not need to chase down the ball.

If he needs two balls, don't hit the second one until he has caught the first one, otherwise he probably won't catch either one. This is not only the courteous thing to do, but it will speed up the game since the players won't be forced to wander around retrieving balls.

The third ball. If the server has two balls and you have the third but do not want to hold it during the point, you should hit it to the back of the court behind the server's partner, the court not being used by the server. He will be going to that court for the next point, and can retrieve the ball at that time.

Ignore the fault. If the first serve is a fault, do not hit it into the net. First of all, it may roll around the court, causing a delay in play when the server is preparing to hit his second serve. Secondly, tennis is a game of muscle patterns, so when you hit the ball into the net, you are practicing that shot and it may come back to haunt you. Just let the first serve go.

Naturally, there will be serves which land too close for you to know whether they are good or out, in which case you will hit and call at the same time. This is acceptable and, as you are trying to return this service, you are not knocking the ball into the net, therefore not developing a poor muscle pattern.

Ignore his feet. In social tennis, there are an enormous number of foot faults and in most cases it's just sloppiness. Even if it seems blatant, you should never call a foot fault on your opponent. In the first place, you really can't see properly from the other side of the court so it's not a friendly thing to do. What's more, if you're so busy concentrating on your opponent's feet, you're not thinking about the right stuff.

Learning proper tennis language and terminology is helpful to everyone and can avoid embarrassment. Here is an anecdote to demonstrate the importance of using proper tennis terms.

While working with two women in a singles lesson, I asked one of them, "What do you do when you hit a ball on the second bounce?" She replied that she would shout over the net, "Oh, that was a double bounce. That's your point." I agreed that if there was no official, she needed to call the balls on her side of the net, but that she shouldn't shout that it was two bounces, that the proper terminology in this situation is "Not up." It is the accepted phrase to use as it is quick, to the point and preferable to a more lengthy explanation.

About a week later this same woman was taking a lesson from my son Jay and she asked him for help.

"Jay," she said, "your Mom was telling us the proper way to call a second bounce on yourself and I can't quite remember the phrase. Was it 'Up yours?' "she wanted to know.

6. RULES

(OR, HOW TO BE MORE POPULAR ON THE
TENNIS COURT)

Knowing and playing by the rules of tennis is vitally important, yet many players are not completely familiar with the rules. Most pro shops carry a Professional Tennis Association booklet with the rules spelled out in detail. Get a copy and commit them to memory.

I will not attempt to define and explain the basic rules in this publication. However, I've decided to include tips about some of the rules which many players seem to find confusing and therefore break unintentionally. I hope the following suggestions and reminders will seep into your subconscious. Observing all the rules, written as well as unwritten, will make you a more popular player.

Let it drop. If a player is standing out of court, behind the baseline or on the outside of the sideline, no matter how far, and his opponent's ball hits him or he catches the ball before it bounces, the opponent wins the point. Always let the ball bounce out.

Change the server. In doubles, *if the server accidentally serves out of turn, his partner should take over just as soon as the mistake is discovered,* even if it's in the middle of a game.

Continue the receiver. On the other hand, *if one player accidentally receives in the improper court, that position is retained until the game is over,* even if the mistake is discovered sooner. When the game is concluded, the players then return to their proper receiving positions.

12-Point Tiebreaker

One even serve. Playing 12-point tiebreakers is confusing to many players. It's very helpful to remember that when the tiebreaker starts, the score is Love-Love, so that the first server will serve into the <u>even</u>, or the forehand, court since the score at that point is <u>even</u>. *The first server of the tiebreaker gets only one serve.*

Two odd serves. Though the first server of the tiebreaker serves only once, *each server thereafter gets two serves.* Therefore, after the first (single) serve into the forehand court, each new server will be starting on an <u>odd</u> score and take the first of his two serves into the <u>odd</u> court, the ad/backhand court.

Six point changeover. Players change sides after every six points in a tiebreaker. Since the first point of a tiebreaker is served into the forehand court and each time the serve rotates to a new player, the serve will be into the uneven, or backhand, court, this means *the player who is serving when the score reaches a total of six points must change to the other side of the net in the middle of his turn. He will then take his second serve into the even, or forehand, court.*

Every little bit counts. If the ball touches the line on the bounce, even just a tiny little bit of the line, *the ball is good!*

White is cool. Before you go to a new club to play, it's a good idea to check to see if they require white tennis clothing. If there is a "white only" rule, it should be honored. Some may think this an old fashioned rule, but it might help to remember that white clothing is cooler than colored clothing. On a hot, humid day you will last longer and feel better if dressed in white.

There are clubs which allow a small amount of colored trim but the amount is generally very limited. Don't try to get around the rules to make a fashion statement.

I have always believed in following rules that are set up for good reasons. Over the years I have had to send people away from the courts because of colored clothing or improper footwear, so I had a reputation for being a stickler.

On one occasion at Martin's Dam Club, a member brought a female guest to play tennis, and it was very noticeable that the guest was braless. That evening, at a dinner party held by one of the club members, the discussion was focused on the female who had played with no bra and one of the dinner guests asked, "Didn't Winnie say anything to her?" The reply was, "Heavens, no. Winnie only checks shoes."

7. SERVING AND RECEIVING

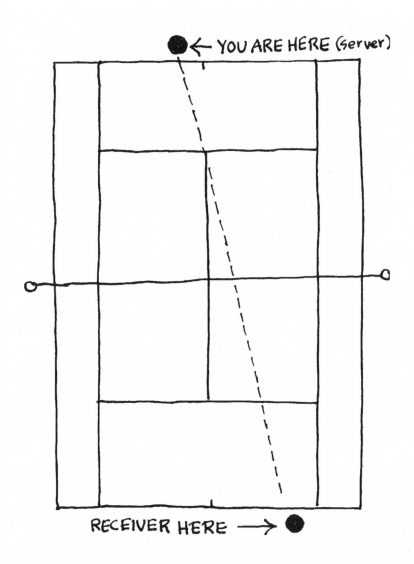

ERVING SETS UP THE GAME

All on your own. The serve is the only shot in tennis in which you are completely on your own; no one has anything to do with that shot except you. You should set yourself up to serve about 6" back of the baseline and get prepared, that is, get physically and mentally set to serve. Take some practice serves if the match is just beginning; when you serve later in the match, take some deep breaths and think about where you will hit the serve.

Pick your spot. Don't just hit your serve "somewhere" in the service box. You should always pick a spot in the service court and try to hit that particular spot. You will then have a point of reference from which to make a correction if the first ball is a fault. If you have nothing to correct from, your control will never get any better.

First serves count. Having a high percentage of successful first serves is the best way to increase your chance of winning a match. Remember that if you find yourself losing, increasing the success rate of your first serves can turn that loss into a win.

Any serve uses a lot of energy so it's very important, physically, to produce a large percentage of first serves, in case you go to a third set. It's also psychologically important to get your first serve in. First-serve success will give you a lift and may help to undermine your opponent's confidence.

If your success rate is not high enough, you need to change something. For instance, try reducing the power on your first serve to 3/4 speed. It's better to reduce your speed and get 75-80% of your first serves in than to hit full power and get only 10% in. You can always go back to full power after you've achieved first-serve success.

If your opponent is receiving well off both the forehand and the backhand, hit the serve directly at him. It will force him to move.

Shifting your weight. When you set up to serve, your back foot should be parallel to the base line with your front foot at a 45° angle to the base line. The imaginary line which can be drawn from toe to toe should be pointing to the middle of the target serving court.

While leaning on your back foot, the ball should be released about 18" in front of you. As you shift your weight from the back to the front foot during the serving motion, you will move forward that distance, about 18", to connect with the ball.

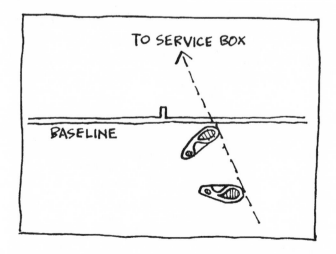

The toss. A very large part of successful serving is ball position. If you can throw the ball the same height and same position into the air with consistency, you are well on your way to being a good server.

Hold the ball with your fingers, not down in the palm of your hand. The motion to put the ball in the air is more like a push than a toss, similar to putting a box onto a shelf that is over your head. Your tossing arm should be at its full extension after the ball is in the air. The ball should not be too high; you should hit the ball at the top of its flight, not have to wait for it to drop down.

Hit out. It's a tennis myth that you should hit *down* on the ball when you serve. Actually, you should have the feeling that you are hitting *up* or hitting *out*, never down. If you hit down, the ball probably will go into the net. In order to literally hit down on the ball, you would have to make contact at a height of about ten feet or higher for a ball to clear the net and land in the service court.

Not too snappy. It is also a tennis myth that you should snap your wrist when you serve. The snap you've heard about comes from the elbow, not the wrist. Where you place the served ball in the court depends on the angle of your racquet face, so if you're snapping your wrist all over the place, who knows where your racquet face will end up!

Stay put. The placement of the serve is determined by the angle of the racquet face. You should not change your body or foot positioning to change the placement of your serve.

Hit deep. The depth of your serve is really more important than its speed. You want to keep the serve very deep.

In singles, most of your serves should go to the *outside* of
the service court but, of course, you should vary the placement. The serve should go wide in singles in order to pull
your opponent out of position.

In doubles, most serves should go to the "T" because it cuts
down on the angled returns. Also, your net man is not pinned
in the alley, having to guard against the down-the-line shot.

 *ERVICE RETURN TIPS*

Cover the angles. As the receiver of a serve, you should
position yourself to bisect the service line with the server. In
other words, if the server stands farther out towards the alley
to serve (which is not a good position for singles serving, but
some players do it), then you must move out closer to the
alley. You must cut that service line in half with the server so
that you have both corners covered.

The depth that you choose to position yourself, of course,
depends on the surface of the court, plus the depth of the
server's ball, the spin of the ball and the speed of the ball. You
want to be far enough back so you're never hurried.

Study your server. Players sometimes have habits that
will help your anticipation. Don't try to do anything fancy on
the service return. Get the ball in play. Don't miss the service
returns or you'll be letting your opponent know he can count
on free points every time he serves to you.

Wait with a backhand grip. The backhand grip is the one you should use as you wait to receive the serve. There are several reasons for this: first, you must meet the backhand earlier than the forehand. If you are waiting with a forehand grip and your opponent serves a powerful serve to your backhand, you may not have time to make a grip change, and it is almost impossible to hit a backhand shot with a forehand grip.

If, on the other hand, you receive a sensational serve to the forehand, leaving you no time to change your grip, you can hit the forehand shot (usually a slice) with a backhand grip. If you are on the defensive, don't try to do anything fancy; just get the ball in play.

CORRECT WAITING POSITION FOR RECEIVING SERVE FOR RIGHT HANDED PLAYER. RACQUET HEAD IN FRONT OF LEFT SHOULDER AND FOREARM PARALLEL TO COURT.

Favor the backhand side. The waiting position is extremely important because your swings all begin from this point. The correct waiting position for a right handed player starts with the right forearm parallel to the court, which puts that hand and the racquet handle at a comfortable distance from the body, waist high. The racquet head should be *in front of the left shoulder, favoring the backhand side*, as the backhand has to be met earlier than the forehand. (Holding the racquet head directly in front of your body puts the racquet halfway between the forehand and backhand which does not favor the backhand.) The left hand should be lightly holding the throat of your racquet.

From a proper waiting position you can make the elliptical swing required (the only continuous swing in tennis) by simply pivoting your body. You don't have to lift the racquet up; it is already at shoulder height so the swing is simplified. You simply drop your forearm down at the back of the swing and bring it forward into the ball. It takes all the variations out of your swing if you start from the same waiting position each time and simply pivot as you bring the racquet around and through this continuous swing.

The waiting position should be the mirror opposite for a left handed player, with racquet head in front of the right shoulder.

Elliptical for top spin. The elliptical swing gives the ball a natural top spin. The stroke begins by a pivoting of the body, thereby taking the racquet head back with the momentum of your body. To hit with topspin, the racquet is lowered below the ball by dropping the forearm, then brought forward through the ball, finishing at shoulder height.

A broken swing, straight back - stop - straight forward, is not nearly as effective as the elliptical swing which is a natural outgrowth of waiting in the proper position.

The service return is vital. There is no bigger psychological lift for the server than when his serve does not come back!! If you miss two service returns in a game, you're saying to your opponent, "Okay, you may start this game at 30-Love," since you've just given the server two free points. So it's vital to get the ball in play.

In singles, content yourself with a deep forehand or backhand crosscourt shot for maximum safety. In doubles, do the same unless the server's partner is leaving his alley *wide* open. If the server is a serve-and-volley player, your service return should bounce at his service line (no deeper) so as he comes rushing towards the net, the ball will be dropping and he will have to volley up.

Use your best return. In club play, the ball crosses the net fewer than five times on the majority of points. This means you'll probably hit the ball no more than three times in the course of a typical point. Getting the ball in play with your most reliable return and then keeping it going with two more shots is likely to win you the point.

Beware the net! As I've mentioned before, your opponent is *not* your #1 enemy - it's the net! Get the ball over it and into the court. You cannot win a point, no matter what, if your ball does not go over the net. Keep the ball in play and let your opponent make the errors. The worst error in singles is to hit the ball into the net, particularly from the baseline. That net is your real opponent in any competitive match.

8. COMPETITION

ears ago, I was called by a father who wanted to hire me to teach his daughter. He said she had had lessons and had very nice mechanics; he wanted me to make her into a competitor. I turned down the assignment because, as I told him, "I don't believe you can teach someone to be a competitor."

I suggested that he should not push her into competitive play but should allow her to play socially and enjoy the game; otherwise he might drive her off the court entirely. Though I do believe that competing is the surest way to improve your concentration and your game in general, there are some who prefer to simply play with their chums without the pressure of a match situation. For many, that's enough, and it's what makes the sport pleasurable. If you do plan to compete, however, here are a few hints.

Compete to improve. Competition is undoubtedly the single greatest activity to help improve your tennis. If you take two people who are evenly matched and put them in a tournament or challenge situation, the one with the most competitive experience will have the edge and will win 9 times out of 10. There is no substitute for this experience.

Think the right stuff. When you are on the court in a competitive situation, you must *never think about your mechanics,* unlike practice sessions when that's all you should think about. With competition, there are *far too many other things on which you should concentrate*:

What is the appropriate shot?

What is your opponent doing?

What is his weakness?

Is he a back court player or does he like the net?

Can he volley?

Does he hit with speed or with spins or both?

Does he move well forward, backwards, sideways?

Does he anticipate?

With these competitive issues in mind, you can't afford to concern yourself with whether you're stroking the ball as you were taught in your last lesson, or whether you have blown an easy point. If you are not thinking ahead to your next shot and concentrating on your opponent, you are thinking about the wrong things.

Think positively. Winning is being able to take a 6-4, 5-4 match and close it out. When you have a "set up," a close out point, instead of thinking "how am I going to avoid missing this point?" you should be thinking "Where am I going to put this ball to win the point?"

As a result of negative thinking, there are a lot of very good players who never learn how to win, how to close out a match. You should always be thinking positively rather than negatively.

The ripple effect. The effect of our thoughts is like the reaction of the water surface when we throw a pebble into a pond. Little ripples start to run out to the edge of the pond, and the ripples grow bigger and bigger. Obviously, you will perform better if that ripple represents a positive, rather than a negative, thought.

Nothing to fear but fear itself. Fear is probably the greatest single thing that restricts stroke production. It is also the reason many players rally better than they play. When you rally, you can't lose a point so you hit the ball without fear.

Of course, under these conditions, you hit your best. But when you are in a game situation, too often you let fear creep into your thoughts: fear that you can't make the shots you would like to make, fear that you can't sustain the rallies, or fear of losing. And fear is generally accompanied by tension. Strokes that should be fluid and smooth become tense and jerky. Fear and tension make your control go right down the tube.

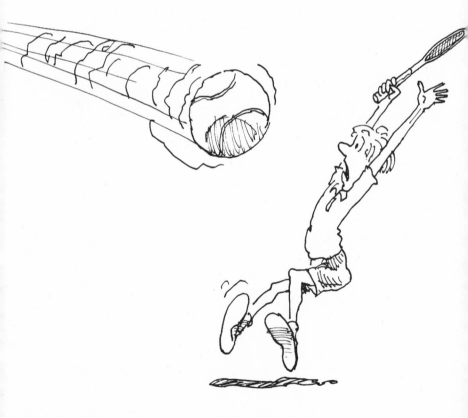

Fear of failure. It is almost always more difficult to compete against someone of lesser ability than yourself. Why? Because you are expected to win, so you walk out on the court being fearful that you might not. There's that old enemy, fear, again! Push it aside by thinking about your game plan and what you perceive your opponent's game plan to be. Banish all those other thoughts, the ones about whether you should win or not.

Think of your game plan. To overcome fear, you must concentrate on *what you are doing and what you plan to do, as well as what your opponent is doing.* That's a lot to think about, but figuring out strategies and planning ahead is how you are going to win. So if you can keep all of these things in your mind, and only these, then you have no room in your thoughts to be fearful.

If you find yourself feeling tense, slowing the pace of the game slightly will help you to focus your thoughts. Take a little more time between points to burn up some of your adrenalin. Breathing deeply through your nose and exhaling through your mouth will help control the rush of adrenalin. When your adrenalin is under control, your emotions will moderate and you will be less tense.

Winning the choice. After the warm-up, as play is about to begin, one of the players will toss his racquet and ask the other to call the toss. With the old wooden racquets, the call was usually "rough or smooth," now it is often "up or down" referring to the letter on the end of the handle. In any case, tossing of a racquet determines who "wins the toss." Though this is known as winning the toss, in essence it is *winning a choice,* because when you win the toss, you have one of four choices:

1. You may choose to serve. Your opponents then may choose the side, and they automatically receive.

2. You may choose to receive. Your opponents then may choose the side, and automatically serve.

3. You may choose the side. Your opponents then may choose to serve or receive.

4. You may require your opponents to make the first choice.

In doubles, if you win the toss, choosing the fourth option can make an important difference as to how the serving will proceed. This option will create *the opportunity for you or your partner to serve first, away from the sun.*

Example: Jane and Barb are a doubles pair. Barb has by far the best serve; the pair wants Barb to be the first server on the team, but Barb *absolutely cannot serve facing the sun.* If Jane and Barb win the toss and require that the opponents make the first choice (#4), Jane and Barb can end up with Barb serving first with her back to the sun. Here's how:

1. If the opponents choose to serve, Jane and Barb *may choose the side facing the sun.* When they switch after the first game, Barb can serve first, with her back to the sun.

2. If the opponents choose to receive, Jane and Barb automatically *become the first servers and may choose the side,* in which case Jane and Barb may choose the court with Barb's back to the sun.

3. If the opponents choose the side, Jane and Barb *may choose either to serve or receive,* depending on the location of the sun.

Two for one. Every player has a strength and a weakness. If you're playing in a competitive situation, the opponent is likely to be a pretty good tennis player; nevertheless, he will probably have a weakness which can be exploited. Early on in a match, you should pay enough attention to figure out that weakness. Then, even though your tendency will be to pound away at that weakness, resist the temptation.

Your best strategy to exploit an opponent's weakness will be to *alternate your shots*, to hit two shots to his strength and one to his weakness. If you keep pounding balls to his weakness, that weakness will improve as the match continues. With two to the strength and one to the weakness, the weakness will not improve much and you'll get more errors from that shot.

Get the first point. The first point of each game is very important. If you win it, work hard for the second point. Then, if you have won the first two points so that the score is 30-0, don't think you're out of the woods. There is real danger of a let-down and a big possibility of losing the next point. Reach deep for that point, concentrate hard and don't allow yourself to be distracted from your goal.

During my years of teaching, and for reasons which I cannot explain, I have heard a great many complaints, primarily from female players, that the drop shot is "unfair." It is perceived as a dumb shot, a lousy shot, as not a good tennis shot. This makes no sense and is really just an excuse for a lack of anticipation. But because of this interpretation, many female players, who think the game should only be played with deep shots to the baseline, are vulnerable to the drop shot. The lob is another shot which is perceived as a lousy shot while, in truth, it is very effective in certain circumstances. Don't be trapped by this false idea.

All's fair. In tennis, the purpose is to hit the ball so your opponent cannot return it. Winning the point is your goal, no matter whether you hit the ball hard, deep, at an angle, down the alley, high in the air, or drop it over the net short. Any shot that cannot be returned is a fair, in fact, a *good* shot. All's fair in love, in war and in making tennis shots.

Change is good. If you're losing, change your game, but stay within the realm of your capabilities. If you are basically a baseline player, don't try to become a net rusher in the middle of a match. Try, instead, to change the spin of the ball or the speed, hit more lobs, hit softer shots, change directions, hit more backhands or forehands. Try to find something you can change when you're losing.

Stay with a winner. Never change your game when you're winning. If you're in a match and are winning most of the points and games, it would be foolish to change whatever it is you're doing. If you've been playing to the forehand with good success, then you should not, all of a sudden, decide to make a change by hitting the ball to the backhand. Don't ever change a winning game.

The very fact that you're winning will make you feel very positive, psychologically, and build your confidence level. It's a little bit like getting the first serve in, which gives you an enormous boost, even if your first serve doesn't really differ from your second serve. In addition, the fact that you don't use nearly as much energy when all of your first serves go in is another advantage, both physically and psychologically.

Dig for the 7th. In competition, unless you win or lose the match 6-Love, the most important game of any set is the 7th game. Reach back for that game. If the score is 3-3, the 7th game puts you ahead 4-3, within 2 games of winning the set, and gives you a boost. If you are at 4-2, the 7th game gives you a commanding lead at 5-2. Conversely, if you win the 7th game when the score is 2-4 against you, the score is then 3-4. You have prevented your opponents from grabbing that commanding lead and pulled yourself back into a position of possibilities. Dig deep for the 7th game.

9. THE TEAM LADDER

he team ladder is important for developing a team to play in a competitive league. The challenges which take place on both the singles' and doubles' ladders are vital for establishing the order of the players on the team, according to ability. In order for the ladder to be accurately set, which is the only way to be fair to both the team players and the opposing teams, *it's important that the challenges be issued and accepted according to established rules.*

Stick to the rules. There are many ways to set up a ladder. I happen to believe it's best to let the team chairman and the team members set the rules for the ladder, with the pro's input. But the most important aspect of any challenge ladder is that the participants and the pro or decision-maker *must never deviate even one tiny little bit from the established rules.* If, at the end of a season, after the challenges are over, the team members are not happy with the rules, the system of challenges can always be changed, adjusted, made more equitable. Simply rewrite the rules. But *during a regular team season, the challenge ladder rules must be followed to the letter.*

To get started. Ladders can be set up in any number of ways. They differ from club to club. To get a ladder started, the pro may simply evaluate the singles players and doubles pairs and arbitrarily place them on the ladder.

When establishing a new ladder, it's not a bad idea to set it up so that anyone on the ladder can challenge at any level above them; #10 pair can challenge #4 if they feel they have been placed in the wrong position and can beat pair #4.

After a season of challenges, when placement on the ladder reflects player's abilities, the pro can place newcomers on the bottom of the ladder and let them challenge anywhere above.

Challenge opportunities. Anyone wishing to play on a competitive team should understand the *opportunity* inherent in challenge matches. They are, of course, necessary in order to establish an accurate ladder. But also, and perhaps even more important, challenge matches are a terrific way for team players to get experience in competing. There is no better way to improve your game than to play in competition. So if you have seven challenge matches during a season, you have added seven matches to your competitive experience.

Unfortunately there are always a few players who lose sight of the reasons for challenge matches and interpret the challenge as a personal attack. A few players I have known over the years, protective of their spot on the ladder, were unable to see the value of playing a challenge which might result in their losing that spot. They construed the challenges as personal, rather than understanding their necessity and value.

Club ladders. The ladders which I have handled for club teams have had different challenge rules than those for school teams. New club players were not placed on the bottom of the ladder, as was the case with school teams.

With a short season, the club ladder had to be established fairly quickly, so new players were given two free challenges onto the ladder and could challenge anywhere they wished. If they lost the first challenge, they could issue their second challenge at a lower level. If they then won a spot, they could still challenge up from there, while having to accept challenges alternately from below. If they lost the second challenge, their name was placed at the bottom of the ladder.

This is a good system, better than if the pro assigns the challenge position. It eliminates the possibility of the new player thinking that he should be challenging higher than the pro has allowed him to. When a player makes the decision himself, the responsibility is on his shoulders alone.

In the case of a fairly decent player, he doesn't have to start all the way at the bottom of the ladder because, with a short season, it would take him too long to reach the level where he belongs. The slow climb from the bottom not only penalizes the individual player, but is also unfair to the teams against which he will be playing if he is too strong to be competing at a lower level, and will penalize his own club's higher team on which he should be positioned.

Alternate challenges. Once on the ladder, club players under my supervision had to alternate the offensive and defensive challenges; they had to accept a challenge from below, before and after each challenge they were allowed to issue to players higher on the ladder. I think this worked very well.

Choose a non-playing arbiter. If you're the ladies' or men's chairman and you play on a team and are a part of the ladder, yet you're making the final decisions about challenges, you're in a no-win situation. There's always someone who's going to believe you are trying to feather your nest.

It is a far better situation when the final arbiter of who may issue and who must accept a challenge is a non-playing person. It should be someone who is not trying to get a place on the team. The pro is probably in the best position to be the decision maker. If the pro is not available for this job, at least the task should fall to someone who is not trying to move up the ladder and, therefore, has no ax to grind.

Make no exceptions! Once the challenge rules have been established, the most important aspect of overseeing the ladder is never to deviate from the rules.

I know of a situation in which the decision-maker deviated from a specific challenge rule, with a chaotic result. The specific rule in effect was that once a challenge was issued and scheduled, with the day and time specified, any change would result in a default. If one person or team was unable to play at the specified time, the person or team which backed out was required to default to the other player or team.

In this case, there was a doubles challenge which had been scheduled, time and day stipulated, and the husband of one of the players died unexpectedly. Of course everyone was upset and sympathetic so, instead of sticking to the rules, the challenge was canceled, and there was no default. (The rules were broken.)

Now, one of the members of that challenging team had planned a skiing trip in Colorado and, before she left, she and her partner set up a challenge to be played when she returned. While she was away, she sprained her ankle very seriously, so that when she returned and could not play she was, according to the rules, expected to default the match. Remembering the case of the woman whose husband died, the injured woman felt she should be given a break because of her sprain, and suddenly there were disgruntled players and tension within the ranks. In this case, had the rules been followed in the first instance, the woman with the sprained ankle would never have questioned her need to default.

The problem came about because an established rule was broken. As unfortunate as it was that one woman lost her husband and another woman sprained her ankle, the overriding rule had been broken, putting the arbiter in the position of having to make a judgment about which of the situations was more serious.

In this example, we know, of course, which was more serious but, for all intents and purposes, the message being sent was that one team had to default because its misfortune was not as great as that of the other team.

If you break the rules for one person, you can break the rules for everyone, no matter the severity of the situation. Once the rules are broken, there is chaos.

School challenges. Within the school teams I coached, I encouraged challenges during every practice throughout the entire season. I never cut challenges off because it was important for the players to build up their competitive experience. Also, kids improve as a season progresses and fairness dictates that the stronger players should be able to move up the ladder. Knowing you are going to lose your seniors each year, this is the way to plan ahead to develop your team for the next year. It's the way to give the younger players a lot of competitive experience.

The varsity positions didn't change during a season because the league rules say that once you've established your team, the lineup must stay the same unless someone's out sick or there's an emergency. But I had a policy of never cutting anyone off the tennis team and, with the large tennis teams which I coached over the years (my last year at one school I coached 52 kids), I let the players below the varsity level have challenges as often as they wanted. We had a lot of challenges!

The whole point is to get the ladder set as accurately as possible according to the ability of the players. That's what a ladder is for. With the school teams, I never broke up the ladder of the returning kids but they were allowed to challenge upwards all season and they moved up according to their abilities. Newcomers were placed at the bottom but could still challenge as far above as they deemed appropriate. Now and then there would be a new kid joining the team who was good enough to beat the #3 person. If, starting at the bottom, he or she had only been allowed to challenge two spots above, it would have taken forever for him/her to reach the proper level.

10. SINGLES

Six steps for Singles, in order of importance:

1. Consistency:

Keep the ball in play. This is your number one priority in any match. Remember, you can only win points if you can keep the ball in the court one shot longer than your opponent does. If you get the ball over the net and in the court after the serve 2 and 2/10 times, you will win about 75% of the points; if you win 75% of the points, you will win *a lot* of matches. When reflecting on a match, people find this statistic hard to believe. They seem to remember only the points which have included long rallies. Memorable as these lengthy exchanges are, they are only worth about 25% of the total points.

2. Depth

Hit deep. Depth in singles is extremely important. Your goal should be to keep your opponent behind the baseline. If your balls are bouncing inside the service line, your opponent will move forward inside the baseline and you'll find yourself in big trouble.

If your balls are bouncing too short, inside or around the service line, you have two possibilities for producing deeper shots: one is to *hit the ball a little higher over the net*; the other is to *hit the ball harder.* You'll make fewer errors if you choose the former, to hit the ball *higher* over the net. Hitting it harder is likely to find you going beyond your capabilities, spraying balls over the baseline.

3. Shot Selection

The straight approach. An approach shot should be hit from a ball which lands 4 or 5 feet or more inside the baseline. When planning an approach shot, don't use a crosscourt shot unless you're sure you can make a winner. If your opponent gets to the crosscourt ball, you're going to be passed. Hitting the ball straight ahead from your position on the court is a far better approach shot since it cuts down on the angles which can be used against you.

Change the pace. If, during play, your opponent is running you around from one side of the court to the other, take a little bit of speed off your ball and hit it just slightly higher over the net, which gives you a little more opportunity to get back into position. If you are pulled out of court, reduce your ball speed or lob, depending how out-of-position you are. This will give you more time to get back into position, which keeps you in the point.

Play it safe. From the baseline, crosscourt shots are the safest because you're hitting over the lowest part of the net into the largest part of the court.

Use the lob. Don't be afraid to use the lob. It's a very effective shot, both offensively and defensively. If you are playing against a net-crowder, an offensive lob, as long as it is deep enough, is very effective. The use of a defensive lob is important to buy yourself some time when you have been pulled out of position.

4. Variety in Speed and Spins

Change the rhythm. If you hit with the same speed and the same spin on each shot, your opponent can very quickly set up a rhythm, returning your shots easily, while gaining confidence. Don't stick to one pattern. Varying the speed of your strokes and changing how much spin you put on the ball will break up your opponent's rhythm, so he is more likely to make errors.

5. Disguise

Timing is everything. Timing where your racquet face meets the ball (as covered in Chapter 2. "Placing the ball through timing") is the best way to disguise your placement of the ball. If your footwork and body position are correct and consistent as you set up to meet the ball, and you are planning your shots based on where your racquet makes contact with the ball, your opponent will never be able to discern ahead of time where the ball will be placed.

The additional benefit to "placing the ball through timing" is that it will force you to watch the ball longer. As long as you remain correct and consistent with your footwork and body position, you will have fewer off-center hits and be steady in your play.

6. Power

Not least, but last. Final, in order of importance, is learning to hit with power. After you have conquered the five previous steps, you can begin to work on power, which is the easiest step to master. Concentrate on good footwork to get pace on the ball, and increase the forward motion of the racquet to increase the ball speed.

11. DOUBLES

I n coaching doubles teams, I always asked: "Do you have someone you'd like to play doubles with?" If two players requested to be paired up, I always agreed. A doubles team is like a marriage. If players are comfortable together, I wouldn't think of interfering. I let them play together even if they didn't seem ideally suited.

If, after a while, a pair was not winning together and was discouraged, I did, on occasion, suggest they consider a change, though I never arbitrarily forced a change. It's very, very difficult to play good doubles if you're not comfortable with your partner. If two players are comfortable together, they will encourage each other and enjoy the game more.

Choose your partner wisely. If you are at the stage in your life where tennis is your #1 priority, it would be a mistake to pick a partner who has tennis lower on his priority list. You will want to practice three times a week while your partner may only have time to play the matches and practice once. You will be frustrated with his lack of commitment; he will be annoyed by your nagging to play more often. Partners should have tennis at the same level on their list of priorities.

Support your partner. In choosing your partner, you'd be wise to pick someone who is supportive, who sees your good shots and overlooks your errors. You must be equally supportive of him. Pointing out each other's mistakes will only serve to undermine one's confidence. No one misses a tennis shot on purpose. Wouldn't it be wonderful if we never made a mistake?

Keep in step. In doubles, remember that you and your partner are not two singles players on the court. All four players are interwoven and what you do and where you go is dependent upon what your partner and your opponents are doing. Moving forward and backward together with your partner is what you must strive for. Imagine that you have a 15' length of rope tied around each waist, stretching from one to the other. In doubles, as in chess, the better you understand the moves, the more enjoyment you will get out of the game.

Check stop. As you're coming to the net, make a check stop just before your opponent hits the ball. If you are still moving forward as the ball comes back over the net, without having made the check stop, you will only be able to hit a ball within your reach. Making that check stop in time will allow you to change directions, giving you wider coverage of the court so you can reach a passing shot.

First serve advantage. Get your first serve in as much as possible. This will give you both a psychological advantage and a physical edge if you find yourself in a long match.

Get to the net. In doubles, your primary goal is to take the net first, before your opponents do. If your opponents gain the net position, you and your partner must never play "one up" and "one back" because your whole middle area will be open for an easy crosscourt put-away. You and your partner also can play aggressively, taking the net position, with all four players at the net together, or you may play in the back court until you see an opportunity. In club doubles, you can play one up and one back all day long if your opponents are playing in this formation or are both playing back. But to play *winning* doubles, you should be aggressive and both move forward to take the net.

Down the middle. Hit the first volley down the middle. This is a good percentage shot and also can promote indecision on the part of your opponents, as they each wonder which of them should take the shot. Never disregard the middle in doubles, whether you're hitting a volley or a ground stroke. Divide and conquer.

Stay in the point. When four or five balls in a row are hit to your partner, it takes a lot of concentration and discipline for you to stay in the point. Though you may have been very alert on the first ball, you are inclined, if you aren't careful, to let down with each successive shot. Staying alert throughout each exchange is a challenge, but extremely important. Force yourself to concentrate and to stay in every point until it's over. Mentally figure that every ball is coming to you so, when and if it does, you are ready.

Avoid the net guy. Hit to the opponent who is the farthest from the net. If the ball is within reach of the net player, that player's job is to hit a finishing volley, and the point should be over. You should always try to hit your shot to the opening, not to the person at the net, even if you think you have a winner.

Don't get into the habit of trying to hit to the sneakers of the net person. Remember that tiny parts of inches on your racquet translate into feet on the other side of the net. At some point, the angle of your racquet face might be just a little bit off, causing you to hit a high ball, in which case the net player will have an easy put-away volley and the point will be lost.

Have a plan. Always have a purpose for every ball you hit. Don't play brain dead tennis with mindless hitting. If you lose because someone is a better player than you, that's understandable and there's no reason to be ashamed or embarrassed. But don't lose because someone is too smart for you.

Think, change your strategy, change the speed and spin of the ball. Have a plan.

Poach. Poaching means moving sideways parallel to the net to cut off a ball that is really your partner's shot. If the poacher does not put the ball away, it is very likely that the poacher's team will lose the point since the poacher's team is now out of position and the opponents should return the ball to the spot that the poacher has left.

How far can the net man go to the center of the court to poach? As far as the opponents will allow! If you're playing against someone who never puts the ball down your alley, then you can go closer to the center of the court, hoping to pick off more volleys. If you find yourself being passed in the alley, then you must move back and protect your territory. The net person's first responsibility is to protect his alley.

Close in for the cut off. When your partner is serving and you are positioned at the net, you should stand in *slightly more than a racquet's length away from the net* during the first serve. If the service return is within your reach, you will be able to connect with the ball above the level of the net, making for an easy put-away volley. If you stand any deeper in the service box, the service return will be dropping by the time it reaches you, forcing you to hit up on the ball, which is seldom a winning shot.

For your partner's second serve, take one or two steps back from the net. Since the second serve is often not as deep or as hard as the first, and the receiver may therefore have stepped a bit closer to the net, your new position will give you more reflex time for cutting off the return shot.

Halfway or side-by-side. Following a successful service return from your opponent, you (the net man) should move back to position yourself about *halfway between the net and the service line* - that is, if your partner (the server) chooses to stay at the baseline (if you're playing one up and one back). If, however, the server (your partner) moves forward to join you at the net, you should move back to play next to him on the service line. *The ideal net position for a doubles pair is side by side on the service line,* prepared to move forward for a volley or backwards for a lob. For best court coverage, doubles partners should move up and back and side to side in unison, as if tied together by a 15' length of rope.

Mid-court advantage. When your partner is receiving serve, you (as his net man) should stand just inside the service box, with your heels in front of the service line. This places you deep enough in the court to make it difficult for the opposing net man to hit behind you. From your position in mid-court, you will have a chance at fielding a crosscourt shot from the net man and staying in the point. If you are closer to the net, the opponent's crosscourt shot will probably go behind you for a winner.

12. HEALTH NOTES

he Warm-up. A proper warm-up consists of gentle stretching and hitting ground strokes, volleys and serves. Muscles can be injured by sudden, jerky movements so the goal of the warm-up is to raise the temperature of your muscles. Tennis players should be particularly aware of the hamstrings, Achilles tendons and back muscles.

When you begin your warm-up, you should hit lightly and groove your shots. You'll gain confidence by being consistent in the warm-up session. You can always add speed gradually later on in the warm-up or after play begins.

Liquids and Salt: New research has shown that cramping is the result of fluid loss, not salt loss. Contrary to former beliefs, perspiration contains very little salt. This means, if play continues on a hot, muggy day, concentration of salt in the blood stream increases because of the way the kidneys work. Putting more salt into the body is unnecessary. The body needs fluid to continue performing at its maximum efficiency.

It's a good idea to drink a glass of water about 1/2 hour before play begins, preferably cold water. Cold water is absorbed faster into the body than tepid water and it also has a desirable cooling effect. A sugary drink before play is not recommended. Once play begins, it's a good idea to drink a cup or two of water on every changeover. Don't wait until you're thirsty because if you've reached that stage, you will be putting the fluids back into your body too late. If you prefer some fruit juice, it should be diluted by half with water.

A hat for heat. Weather with high humidity is the most dangerous for players. If you are involved in a long match, there are several precautions you can take to ward off heat exhaustion. It is very improtant to wear a hat to keep the sun from beating down on the top of your head, particularly when it is hot and humid. A visor will eliminate glare but it won't help to keep your body cool. You should learn to wear a hat that covers the top of your head.

You may think you are uncomfortable with a hat and believe that a hat will be so bothersome and distracting that you'd be better off without it. But being hatless on a sunny, humid day is a great mistake, so get used to wearing one. Practice with a hat on, not just a visor, so that a hat becomes part of your tennis attire. Then, on a muggy day, you will be able to last longer on the court without being affected by the heat.

A cold towel. Cool a towel with ice water, wring the excess water out of the towel and put the cool towel around your neck on the changeover to help keep your body temperature down. Perspiration is the most important heat regulator because the evaporation process helps keep your skin cool. When it's humid, however, perspiration doesn't evaporate as readily so your body temperature is more likely to stay elevated. Try the cool towel trick and continue to drink water. The very best prevention for heat prostration is the steady intake of fluids. It is important to drink continually throughout a match, not waiting until you feel thirsty.

Fluids and shade. Warnings of heat exhaustion include chills, headaches and nausea. If any of these symptoms occur, a player should leave the court for a shaded area and take plenty of fluids. Heat stroke usually is indicated by warm, dry skin and a cessation of perspiring. Symptoms can include a high fever and mental confusion.

Proper first aid for heat exhaustion requires getting the player into the shade, offering plenty of fluids, and administering cold compresses or ice massage. The very best antidote, of course, is for the affected person to recognize the symptoms and to get off the court and into the shade as soon as possible. Be smart. If any heat related problems develop, don't remain on the court in order to not "let your partner (or team) down." This is a dangerous situation and not worth risking your health.

Ice a sprain. If you have trouble with a strain or sprain, you want to get ice on it and elevate it as soon as possible.

Tension relief. It's hard to play percentage tennis if you are filled with tension. To relieve physical tension, play every point hard, take deep breaths through your nose and exhale through your mouth. If you're feeling mentally tense, slow the pace of the match by taking a little longer between points and between games. Don't stall, just slow down a little. Focus, keep your eyes on the ball longer, increase your concentration and run hard during each point.

Tennis elbow. This painful ailment can be prevented easily by gripping the racquet properly. I recently read an extensive article about tennis elbow which, to my horror, never mentioned the greatest single cause of this awful, painful ailment - what I call "long on the racquet," meaning having the heel of your hand either at the very end of the grip or hanging off the end of the grip. There was even a picture with the article which showed a player with a "long on the racquet" grip. I was horrified, and probably should have written a letter to the editor, because I firmly believe that gripping the racquet properly will prevent elbow pain.

I have given *hundreds* of lessons to people specifically because they were suffering from tennis elbow and looking for a solution. Some of these painful elbows are so bad that people can't even pick up a coffee cup. Every single student who has come to me to correct this problem, that is *every single one*, has either had his hand flush with the end of the grip or had the end of the racquet up inside the palm. *Yet I have never seen it mentioned in an article.*

A "long on the racquet" grip is sure to cause tennis elbow eventually because all the weight of the racquet is too far away from the gripping hand. If you play against a hard hitter while using a "long grip," the ball will knock the face of the racquet back, which will knock your wrist back, putting tension on the forearm and sending shock waves reverberating all the way up to the elbow.

Very often, if you choke up on the grip and get the butt of the racquet outside the heel of the hand, you will have taken care of the problem and your tennis elbow with clear up. If this grip change isn't the complete solution, then the muscles of the forearm are undoubtedly in spasm. Getting some massage for the forearm and combining that therapy with shortening up the grip on the racquet almost always clears up a painful tennis elbow.

Playing with a shorter grip and squeezing the grip at the start of your backswing will produce a solid sounding shot, the kind with a nice crack to it. An added bonus to shortening the grip will be increased consistency in your play.

I find it incomprehensible that this bit of information is not widespread. A great deal of pain could be avoided with a simple understanding of how to grip the racquet.

13. FINISHING THE POINT

I hope I have convinced you that tennis is the sport for a lifetime, a great game at any age or stage in your life, a game for camaraderie, healthy exertion, mental challenge, and fun.

A friend or two, a willing spirit, some balls, a racquet and a court are the only requirements - though you soon will have many, many more friends if you are eager and show up at the court often. Millions of people are playing tennis these days. Courts are available everywhere - public and private - and committed players are always looking for a good game, a willing substitute or a partner. Like a fourth for bridge, you'll be in demand if you show enthusiasm and play by the rules. Arrive on time, properly attired, bring along your best manners and a sense of humor, call the shots fairly, learn the unwritten rules and traditions outlined in these pages, and your phone will be ringing off the hook.

If you need more convincing, perhaps some persuasion from a higher power might do the trick. A friend recently told me that tennis is the sport that God likes best. When I inquired why, she replied "Because it's the only sport with Love in it."

So, now, the ball is in your court.

ABOUT THE AUTHOR

Winnie Gilliford is a prominent, well-respected name in Philadelphia area tennis circles. She has taught individual players and coached teams of all sizes, ages, sexes and abilities for 57 years. Her contribution to the world of tennis is immense.

Winnie's ability to diagnose a tennis problem and articulate a solution has had students flocking to her for lessons for years. She has worked with hundreds of players of all abilities, moving some from beginning status to confident team players while helping others to improve an established championship game. Her 'people skills' are as legendary as her tennis prowess. Few people have as many friends. One former pupil gushes, "she possesses all the qualities of royalty - beauty, grace, patience, endurance and savvy."

Winnie began life with physical difficulties which might have discouraged a less staunch individual. Born with congenital back problems, she learned early about a regimen of exercise and therapy to minimize her disabilities. She credits her mother, who she says "raised the child, not the disability," with exposing her to physically challenging sports and encouraging her to try everything. Her involvement with tennis began at the age of 13 as a therapeutic measure.

When Winnie joined the United States Professional Tennis Association (USPTA) in 1963, there was only one other female member in the Middle States division. Winnie was the 12th registered woman professional nationally.

Her first job as a club professional was at the Martin's Dam Club where she established herself as the reigning guru of the tennis world and the 'grand dame of the tennis deck.'

With court reservations disallowed, Winnie made it her responsibility to introduce players to one another and to arrange games with people of more or less equal abilities. An amazing facility for names and faces and an understanding of players' ability levels helped to endear Winnie to everyone.

Winnie's strategy sessions, with blackboard and chalk in hand, are legendary and so sought after, that she has raised money for many non-profit organizations by selling her Chalk Talks as an auction item. Her name is evoked constantly in friendly games, with players reminding each other what Winnie would have them do in a particular situation.

Winnie spent 16 years at Martin's Dam before being wooed away to the historic Merion Cricket Club to serve as the Head Professional and Athletic Director, a prestigious job for anyone, but a bright feather in the cap of a woman. Winnie takes great pride in being part of the recorded history of Merion. The club had never hired a female head professional for any of its racquet sports, and still has not since Winnie's retirement. Winnie served at the Merion Cricket Club for eight years, retiring in 1984.

In addition to Winnie's club assignments, which included being the first professional at Waynesborough Country Club and six years coaching Haverford Tennis Club, she also has coached suburban Philadelphia college and high school teams, beginning with Eastern College men and women. Following retirement from Merion, she worked with disabled and wheelchair tennis players for six years, coached the Villa Maria Academy tennis team for ten years, with one-year stints coaching Linden Hall girls and Radnor High School boys.

Her awards over the years go far beyond tennis. Winnie has been honored repeatedly for her civic work and her work with the disabled.

Winnie Gilliford during one of her well-known, blackboard strategy sessions, referred to by her students as Chalk Talks.

Photo by Linda Walters

Use this page to order by mail.

Name_____

Address_____

City_____State_____Zip_____

Please send me:

WINNIE'S WISDOM
GREAT TENNIS TRUTHS FROM AN 'OLD' PRO

No. of books at $12.50 each _____ $_____

PA residents 6% sales tax (.75 per book) $ _____

Postage and handling * $ _____

      Total: $ _____

* Add $2.50 per book postage and handling

Send check or money order (no cash or CODs) to:

Crawford Press
282 Bluffview Drive
Lancaster, PA 17601

Prices subject to change without notice
Valid in the U.S. only
All orders subject to availability